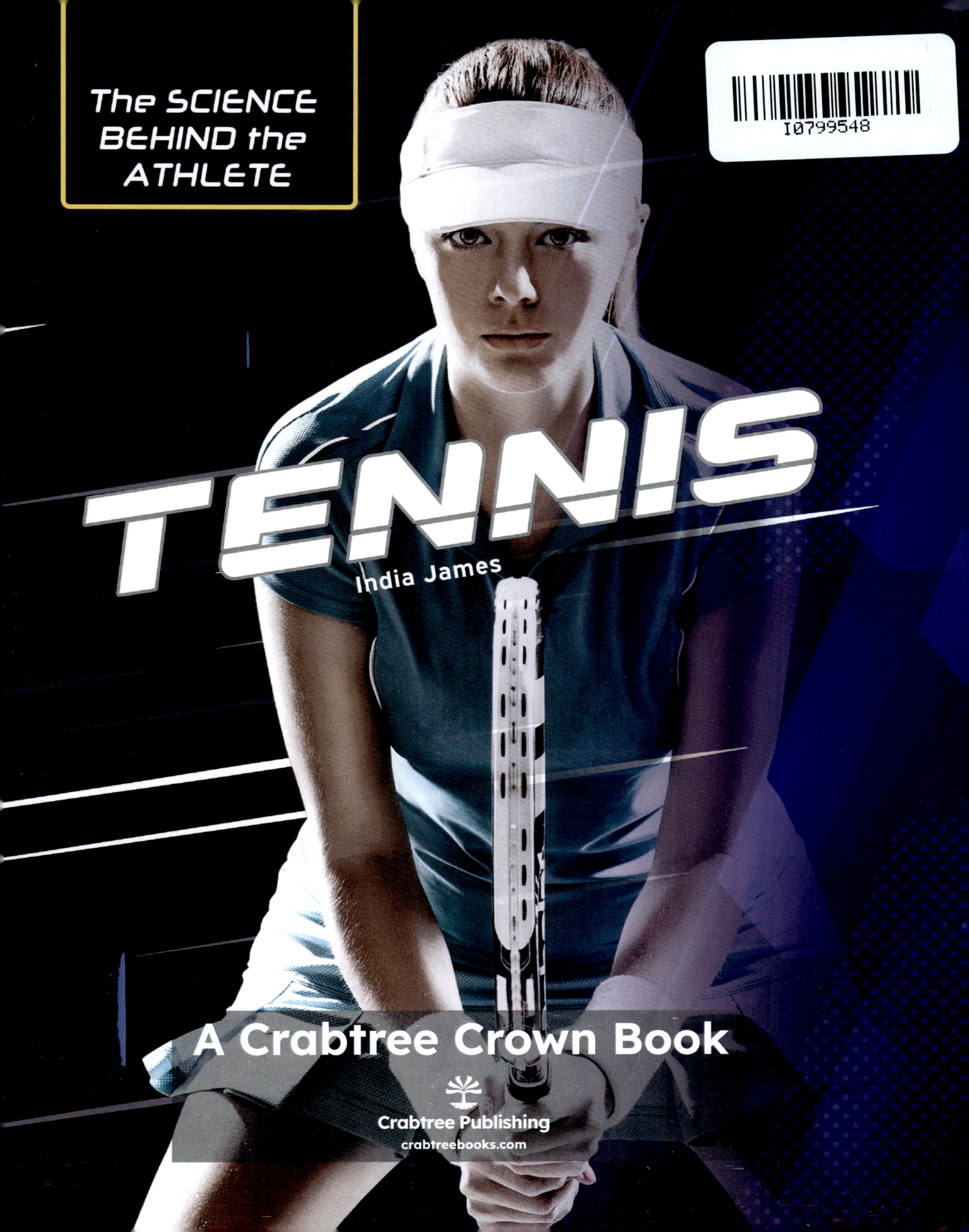

The SCIENCE BEHIND the ATHLETE

TENNIS

India James

A Crabtree Crown Book

Crabtree Publishing
crabtreebooks.com

School-to-Home Support for Caregivers and Teachers

This appealing book is designed to teach students about core subject areas. Students will build upon what they already know about the subject, and engage in topics that they want to learn more about. Here are a few guiding questions to help readers build their comprehensions skills. Possible answers appear here in red.

Before Reading:

What do I know about tennis?

- *I know tennis is a sport.*
- *I know tennis players use rackets.*

What do I want to learn about this topic?

- *I want to know what the first tennis balls were made of.*
- *I want to learn how science is helping players train.*

During Reading:

I'm curious to know...

- *I'm curious to know how tennis balls are made.*
- *I'm curious to know how tennis courts have changed.*

How is this like something I already know?

- *I know players use tennis balls.*
- *I know players play on courts.*

After Reading:

What was the author trying to teach me?

- *The author was trying to teach me what tennis balls are made of.*
- *The author was trying to teach me how technology has changed rackets in tennis.*

How did the photographs and captions help me understand more?

- *The photographs helped me understand how science has improved tennis.*
- *The captions gave me extra information about the history of tennis.*

TABLE OF CONTENTS

WHAT IS TENNIS?

Millions of people play tennis every year. It is a game where **rackets** are used to hit a ball back and forth over a net. A player wins points when their opponent can no longer return the ball within the **court**. Sometimes tennis is played with two people on each team.

TENNIS TRIVIA

It is believed that tennis came from a game played by French **monks** in the 12th century. Some historians believe that the game can be traced back even further—to the ancient Egyptians, Greeks, and Romans!

1

TENNIS RACKETS

RACKET DEVELOPMENT

Tennis was a popular game in Europe by the 1300s. This early game wasn't played with a racket though. Tennis players used their hands to hit the ball back and forth.

TENNIS TRIVIA

The name tennis is thought to have come from the French word tenez, meaning "to hold" or "to take." The French monks used to shout this word when they **served** the ball.

Hitting the ball injured players' hands. So they began using gloves to hit the ball. Then they started using wooden paddles.

During the 1800s, tennis rules and courts changed to become the game we know today. Rackets changed a lot too.

Tennis players, around 1890

WOOD RACKETS

Rackets in the 1800s were made with a solid wood frame. The frame was strung with string made from animal guts. These first gut strings were made from sheep's intestines.

Wooden tennis racket strung with gut strings

sheep intestine

Laminated wood rackets were first used in 1947. They were made with many thin layers of wood that were glued together. This technology made the rackets more durable and lighter than solid wood.

METAL RACKETS

Metal rackets began to be used in the 1960s. The first metal rackets were made of steel. Aluminum and graphite were also used as technology improved. Because these materials were lighter, rackets could be bigger without being too heavy. Oversized rackets were first used in 1976.

TENNIS TRIVIA

A lighter, wider racket makes it easier for tennis players to hit the ball.

RACKETS TODAY

Today, rackets are made from many different materials. Sports companies compete with each other to see who can make the lightest, most durable, strongest racket.

Some rackets are still strung with gut strings made from cows' intestines. Other rackets use strings made of **synthetic** materials. Some players like using rackets that have a combination of the two, with some strings made from gut and some made with synthetic materials.

2 TENNIS COURTS

REAL TENNIS

The first tennis courts were much smaller than today's courts. Players bounced a heavy ball off of walls. They played on a narrow court that was often indoors. This version of the game came to be known as "real tennis."

TENNIS TRIVIA

In 1600, there may have been as many as 1,800 indoor courts in Paris, France.

LAWN TENNIS

In the 1800s, people began playing tennis on lawns outside. This form of the game became known as "lawn tennis." Early games were played on hourglass-shaped courts. Lawn tennis became the version of tennis most commonly played today.

Lawn tennis, 1887

TENNIS TRIVIA

In the 1800s, there were plenty of flat, grassy courts, because these areas were already used for games of croquet.

TODAY'S COURTS

The first tennis tournament at Wimbledon was held in 1877. The people organizing the tournament decided not to use an hourglass shape for their courts. They made rectangular courts instead. The **dimensions** of the courts used today are almost the same as the ones used in this first tournament.

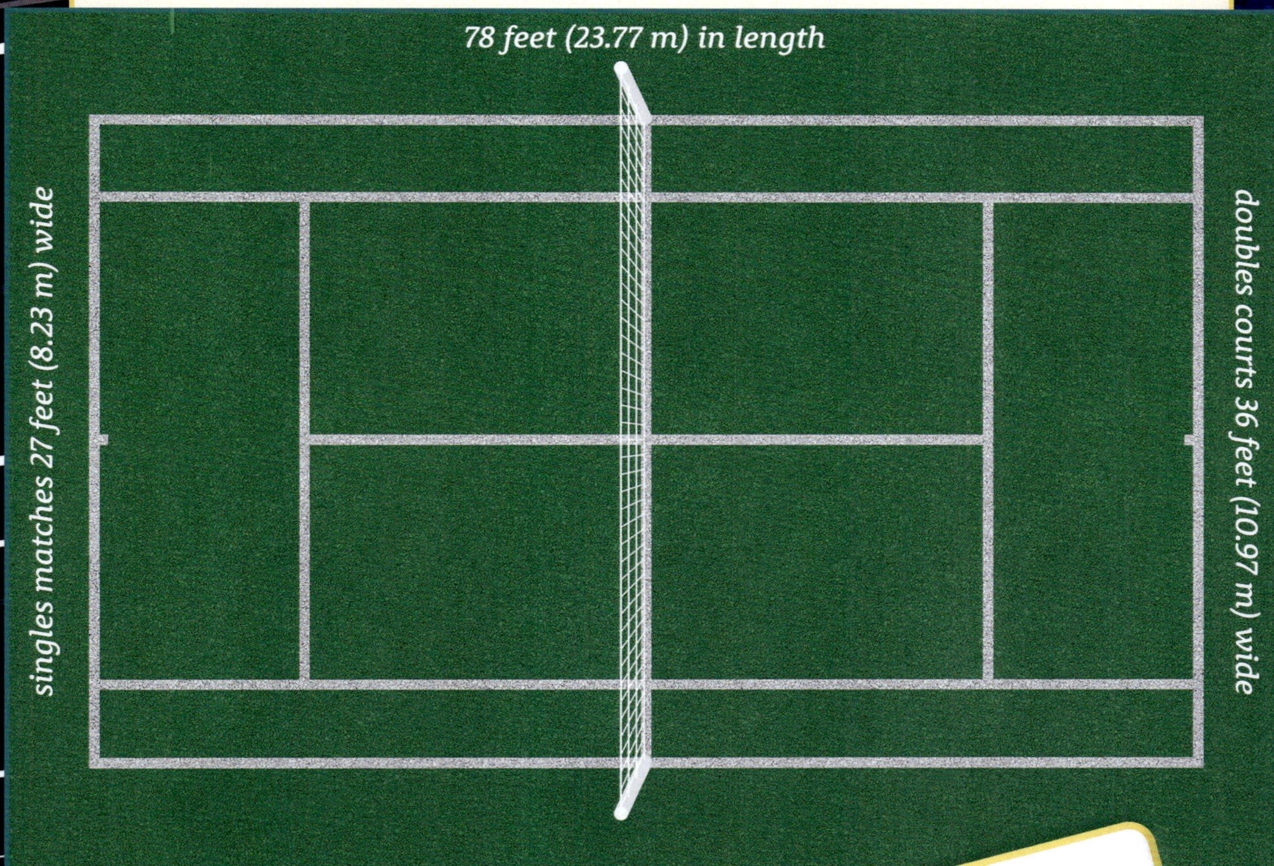

Standard measurements for a tennis court today

TENNIS TRIVIA

Wimbledon is the oldest tennis tournament in the world.

TYPES OF COURTS

Tennis may be played on many different surfaces. Grass courts are the most traditional courts. Tennis balls bounce more unpredictably on these courts. Clay courts can be red or green. Balls tend to bounce high on these courts. Hard courts are made from a variety of different materials including resin, rubber, sand, synthetic, and acrylic. Balls tend to bounce high on these courts as well.

synthetic court

clay court

3 TENNIS BALLS

EARLY TENNIS BALLS

The first tennis balls were very different than the balls used today. The outer shell was made of leather or cloth. The ball was stuffed with rags or horsehair.

horsehair

RUBBER TENNIS BALLS

Tennis balls changed when lawn tennis was created in the 1800s. **Vulcanized rubber** had recently been invented. This material began to be used to make tennis balls.

It was discovered that the balls would play better when wrapped with flannel material. This also helped the balls last longer.

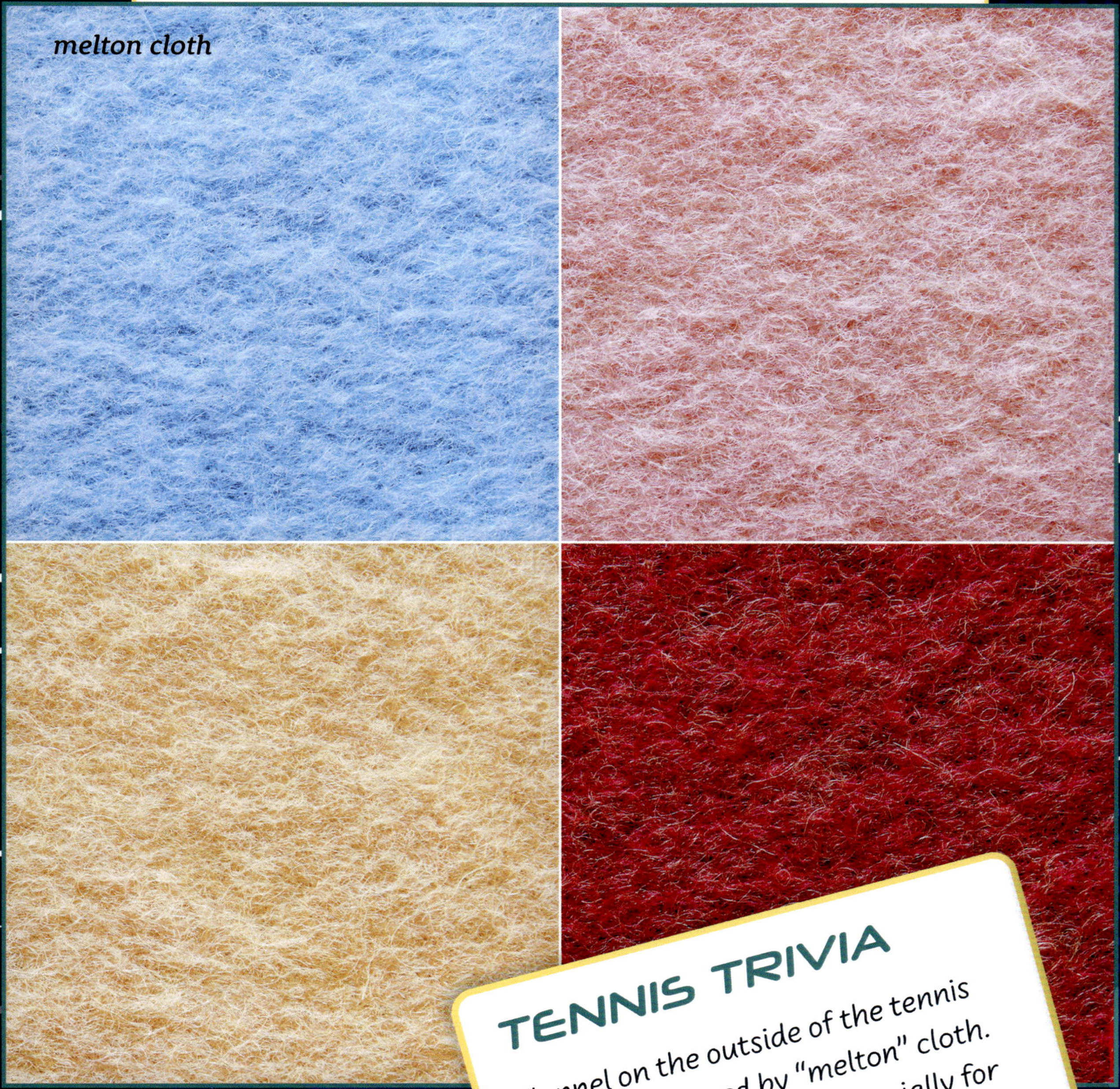

TENNIS TRIVIA

Flannel on the outside of the tennis ball was replaced by "melton" cloth. This is a material made specially for covering the outside of tennis balls.

TODAY'S TENNIS BALLS

Today, tennis balls are no longer solid rubber. At the factory, rubber is molded into two half-spheres. The half-spheres are hot when they are brought together. Pressurized air is forced between the two halves. This gives tennis balls their bounce.

TENNIS TRIVIA

The Wilson Sporting Goods company makes more than 100 million tennis balls each year.

The first tennis balls were white or black. When games started to be shown on TV, the color of the balls changed. Yellow was easier for people watching games on TV to see.

TENNIS TRIVIA

The Wimbledon tennis tournament was the last major tournament to switch from white tennis balls to yellow. Players began using yellow tennis balls at Wimbledon in 1986.

4 TENNIS TRAINING

TYPES OF TRAINING

Training for tennis combines strength training workouts with workouts that raise the player's heart rate. Lots of time on the court helps players practice their technique.

TENNIS TRIVIA

The longest tennis match was played at Wimbledon in 2010. It lasted 11 hours and 5 minutes.

MOTION CAPTURE

Serious players may use **motion capture** to improve their game. Motion capture is a technology that is used in some movies to make special effects. The same technology helps tennis players study their movements. Players wear a special suit and **infrared** cameras record how players swing and hit the ball. Computers take this recording and **analyze** how the player was moving.

Coaches and players can look at the recorded movements in 3-D. They can slow down the recording and examine it from many angles. Looking at how a player moved in detail can help coaches work with players to improve their form.

RECREATIONAL PLAYERS

Even recreational players can use technology to understand how they move and play. There are companies that make small sensors that can be attached to the bottom of rackets. These sensors can help a tennis player understand how fast, how hard, and what motions they use to hit the ball.

5 STATISTICS

Serves and swings might be the most exciting parts of the game, but tennis is a sport that depends a lot on math. **Statistics** is one area where math is used to help understand the game.

STATISTICS

Statistics is an area of math that collects, organizes, and analyzes sets of numbers. In tennis, statistics are used to explain how players are performing. Coaches, scouts, and the media all use statistics to understand how players are performing.

TENNIS STATISTICS

PLAYER 1	6-4 6-3 6-7 MATCH TIME: 2:20	PLAYER 2
7	ACES	6
0	DOUBLE FAULTS	1
6	1st SERVE IN %	45
80	1st SERVE PTS WON %	74
56	2nd SERVE PTS WON %	44
15	WINNERS	19
12	UNFORCED ERRORS	12
8/9	NET POINTS WON	3/13
2/6	BREAK POINTS WON	3/5

Example of statistics from a tennis match

FIRST-SERVE PERCENTAGE

The serve starts a point in tennis. Players are allowed two tries to start the ball for each point. The first-serve percentage is a measure of how often the first try is in the correct spot on the court.

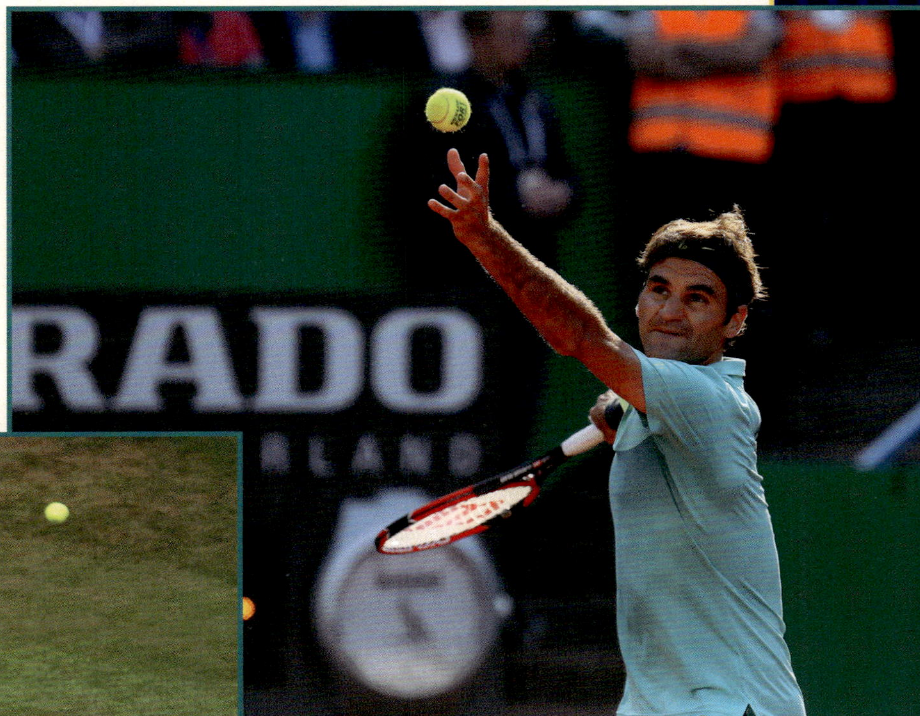

TENNIS TRIVIA

The average of the professional tennis players with the highest first-serve percentages is around 70%.

SERVICE POINTS WON

The service points won is the number of times a tennis player wins the point when they have served. This includes first-serve and second-serve points won. This information can be collected over a season or a player's career.

SECOND-SERVE POINTS WON

Tennis players are allowed two tries to serve. Their second serve is important. This statistic measures how many times a point is won on the second serve.

BREAK POINTS SAVED AND CONVERTED

A break point is when the player returning the serve can win the game with the next point. Break points saved and break points converted are statistics that describe how players perform in that situation.

The more information a person has, the better their statistics will be. Coaches, scouts, and players all use statistics to find out where improvements can be made.

CONCLUSION

Tennis players are athletes that play a fast and exciting game. The rackets, courts, and balls have changed since the first time tennis was played. Science and technology can help make the sport more exciting and safer in the future.

GLOSSARY

analyze (AN-uh-lize): To examine carefully and in detail

court (kawrt): The area that a game of tennis is played on

dimensions (dih-MEN-shuhns): The length, width, height, or depth used to describe an object

infrared (in-fruh-RED): Producing or using rays of light that are invisible to human eyes

monk (mungk): A member of a religious community of men

motion capture (MOH-shuhn KAP-cher): Technology that records movement using infrared light

racket (RAK-it): A piece of sports equipment consisting of a long handle attached to a round frame with a system of tight strings stretched over it

serve (surv): The motion of throwing a ball in the air and hitting it over the net to put a tennis game in play

statistics (stuh-TIS-tiks): A branch of math that collects, organizes, and analyzes numbers

synthetic (sin-THET-ik): A material formed by humans rather than by nature

vulcanized rubber (VUHL-kun-nahyzd RUHB-er): A type of rubber that has been hardened to make it last longer

INDEX

COMPREHENSION QUESTIONS

1. When did people begin playing lawn tennis?
    a. 1900s
    b. 1800s
    c. 1700s
2. Which material was used in the first tennis balls?
    a. horsehair
    b. rocks
    c. sheep gut
3. What is an example of a statistic measured in tennis?
    a. jump height
    b. timed 100-yard dash
    c. service points won
4. **True or False:** Math is important in tennis.
5. **True or False:** Tennis rackets have always been made of the same material.

Answers: 1. B, 2. A, 3. C, 4. True, 5. False

ABOUT THE AUTHOR

India James writes about science, technology, and math for young readers. She loves when science comes together with sports. India lives in Ohio with her family.

Written by: India James
Designed by: Kathy Walsh
Series Development: James Earley
Proofreader: Melissa Boyce
Educational Consultant: Marie Lemke M.Ed.

Photographs: Shutterstock; Cover & Title pg: Mike Orlov, Lilo Alfonso, geen graphy, your; p 2-31 backgrounds: Lilo Alfonso, your; pg numbers: gomolach; p 4: Chen WS; p 5: @Wiki; p 6: Library of Congress, P&P; p 7: Dinoman, Photology 1971; p 8: Steve Collender, mediadrumworld/TopFotoviaNewscom; p 9: Wojciech_Zalewski, Ostill is Franck Camhi; p 10: guruXOX; p 11: @Wiki, Jonathan Park; p 12: Library of Congress; p 13: Shu Ba; p 14: Adam Villimek, Marko Poplasen; p 15: nito, Issarawat Tattong; p 16: Patsaya Chalatichatkul; p 17: ArtKio; p 18: @Wiki, mohd kamarul hafiz; p 19: Mai Groves, Leonard Zhukovsky; p 20: Microgen; p 21: Bruno de CarvalhoviaNewscom; p 22: Rawpixel.com, hedgehog 94; p 23: Coolang, Elmur; p 25: photoyh, Maja HitjvisNewscom; p 26: Young Ho; p 27: Scott StuartvisNewscom; p 28: Jose Luis ContrerasvisNewscom

Crabtree Publishing

crabtreebooks.com 800-387-7650

Printed in Canada/012024/CP20231127

Published in Canada
Crabtree Publishing
616 Welland Ave.
St. Catharines, Ontario
L2M 5V6

Published in the United States
Crabtree Publishing
347 Fifth Ave
Suite 1402-145
New York, NY 10016

Library and Archives Canada Cataloguing in Publication
Available at Library and Archives Canada

Library of Congress Cataloging-in-Publication Data
Available at the Library of Congress

Hardcover: 978-1-0398-3896-3
Paperback: 978-1-0398-3981-6
Ebook (pdf): 978-1-0398-4055-3
Epub: 978-1-0398-4127-7